Some Scattered Pearls

Asit Ghosh

wisdom tree

ISBN: 81-86685-87-1

Published by
Wisdom Tree
C-209/1 Mayapuri-Phase-II
New Delhi-110064
Tel: 28111720,28114437

Printed at
Print Perfect
New Delhi-110064

To Debasmita and Ramanuj, my daughter and son, as an attempt to compensate for my imperfections

ning and ends with the profound wisdom that there is no conclusion. Every learning begin

different streams look alike but are dif

Incidences are similar but experienc

Acknowledgements

Had it been a book on skills and methods for living a valuable life, I would have learnt it from some specialist. Since this book is about life, it is difficult to list those far too many people who have influenced my thoughts and with whom I have swum the stream of life.

When I was five-years old, my parents engaged a tutor to teach me my school lessons. Named Prasanta Majumdar, it was he who introduced me to Rabindranath Tagore's Shishu Bholanath. Interestingly, though this piece was not a part of my school syllabus, my tutor would look for opportunities to read out the poems, teach me their meaning and help me recite the verses. I don't have words to express my gratitude to this first teacher who laid the true foundation for my education in the early days of my life.

My father, as a civil servant, worked in a difficult department. His profound honesty, tolerance, sacrifice and simple living inspired me the most. My mother has been a fountain of love, whose efforts to keep me healthy and happy, especially when I was devoting most of my time to this book, have been my greatest blessings.

Once I lost hope and thought that I had made a mess of my life; I then decided to access the books written by Dr Wayne Dyers. His profound masterpiece, called You will See It When You Believe It, threw open new horizons for me. Soon I came in contact with Mr Aporesh Acharya, formerly of Dale Carnegie Institute, and became his close ally. Through him I opened new doors of spiritual awakening.

Then there were many friends of exceptional quality and character who stood by me like pillars. Among them I wish to mention specially Suchitra Mitra, Dr Shabnam Johry, Sushobhan Mukherjee and Chaitali Nandy. They did everything to look after my daily needs besides reading, writing and listening to my scripts and exercising profound tolerance over my intolerance, arrogance and eccentricities.

Finally, I am grateful to my charming assistant Anjali Savita for making the book possible. Above all the other things, she travelled with me, typed the script, created the cover and the sketches. Her sharp sense of accuracy, understanding, depth and conceptualisation is of extraordinary quality and which gave the form to this book just as I had conceptualised.

Divinity can be a source of self-realisation only. It is a way which is intrinsically beyond logic. It is a way of faith. Faith has a logic that is certainly beyond an ordinary perception. Divinity comes through faith and faith alone. Divinity itself is a quest for self-realisation and nothing more, nothing less.

Attaining purity of thoughts is the ultimate aspiration of a spiritually awakened mind. It strikes me today, while meditating, that even prayer is only an interim stage of evolvement. At the highest level, prayer would be replaced by absolute faith. When there is undaunted faith, prayer ceases to be. Even faith, though higher than prayer, should be an intermittent phase; for, when the urge to surrender comes, even faith mingles into this highest level of a spiritual mind.

When you express from the surface of your mind, those expressions are called statements; but when you express from the depth of your mind, they become quotations. Statements are short lived but quotations live through time and space.

I was turned around from the gutters by the greatest universal prayer:

'Tamaso-ma jyotiramaya
Asato-ma satgamaya
Mryitorma amritamgamaya'

Wonderful and unfathomable have been the ways of this prayer. At times, the most difficult of situations was conquered. What seemed impossible became possible. The transformation was not easy, but highly turbulent. However, the results were astoundingly rewarding. So I am convinced that when nothing works, prayers do.

We often say 'we are one', but remain separated. This is a myth. How can we say that we are 'one', when we are actually 'separate'? Will an undivided orange or a coconut say that we are one? In the first place they, at that level, don't have a concept of 'we'. 'We' are 'we' and can't be 'one'.

It is healthier to say that 'we are together as two individuals'. This is peaceful, pragmatic and most meaningful. The whole Universe operates on this beautiful principle. So long as the whole world is there, many entities will be there, but the fact that remains glorious is the existence of a common harmony among them.

Sin is not in action; it is in reaction! This is indeed an enlightening thought. Volumes can be written on this. Every action tends to leave an impact on the mind. This happens because most minds are not alert or aware. They are without any rapport with the intelligence. The mind that is isolated or separated will register an after-effect of an action. This is because the subconscious mind steals information when the conscious mind is not alert. The subconscious mind is only a process house. This is the database which works on the basis of the past activities. The subconscious mind can also be called the reactive mind. It will bring back the recorded data in various forms to the conscious mind. This causes suffering, pain and repentance. What is hate other than a conscious suffering? Sin is, indeed, a reaction.

Mediocres have a greater subconscious influence on their lives. The special ones are more conscious, and more alert. They operate at the higher level of the mind; the mind that is under the influence of intelligence is called the higher mind. If one does an act consciously and is aware of it — 'Yes I am doing it; I am seeing myself doing it; and I am accepting my action at this present moment' — then the attitude is one of action that is free from reaction. This is the only attitude that fosters growth and evolution. This mind is free from any impact, any past or future. This is a flowing mind for which only the present moment is true — there is no reference. This is the highest level of intelligence — intelligence called awakened intelligence — a very lively, enthusiastic mind, full of vigour, vitality, alertness, potential and creative power.

Neither 'intelligence' nor 'emotion' alone is useful in this world. A rapport between the two is the key to success. Caring is important but unless we are able to care for others with a bonafide purpose, it is of no avail. Love activated into benevolence becomes eternal.

Relaxation can be of two types: external and internal. When both meet at a point, then it is called meditation. A mind full of internal chaos will fail to discover peace even in the most serene of the places. One must prepare one's mind before going on a retreat.

Kindness is above board. To be good is one thing but to be kind is even higher. If you see someone who is not 'kind' enough, don't call him bad because he still could be 'good'. He has not yet evolved to reach the realm of kindness or nobleness but because he is good, he is most likely to reach there soon.

The word 'top' is a misnomer. It means different things to different people. However, to most it means a position — the external perspective. To a few it means a feeling of being on 'top of the world' — an internal perspective. The former is a quantitative pursuit and the latter is a qualitative phenomenon. The risk with the quantitative pursuit is that without the involvement of its qualitative counterpart, it cannot sustain. The advantage of qualitative pursuit is that it is more liberalised and independent than the other. The way to the top needs to be a 'middle path', encompassing both the perspectives.

Ego* and laziness can't be got rid of by soft words or counselling. That's why they are the best partners and always stay together. Wherever you find ego, you will find laziness. One has to strike very hard at them with, not intelligent words of advice, but by adopting harsh methods to crush and shatter them.

* 'Ego' is used in the Indian sense of 'ahamkar' here.

Ego is an unqualified expression of authority. When you attain due authority on a subject, you can control the situation based on your hard-earned knowledge, experience or wisdom. This is not ego. When you are unable to accept the authority of someone well established in a field different from yours, based on your own assessment, then you are a victim of ego.

Ego contravenes knowledge and growth. It emanates from lack of 'shraddha' (faith) or humility. In the Indian tradition of ancient education in 'gurukula', gurus took hard measures, including making their disciples run errands, perform menial and non-specific activities before the disciples became entitled to true wisdom.

I wear two hats. I am trying to attain a tuning between two opposite kinds of traits. My role as an entrepreneur is apparently different from that of a facilitator but I have to, for obvious reasons, house these two different characteristics in me. Fortunately, I am able to achieve a kind of congruence between the two traits and am now able to build more on the basis of the two.

My role of an entrepreneur is a more tolerant and patient one than what I can afford as a trainer. As a trainer I need to push a little harder for I could not let loose and wait. I have to set rather high standards and motivate my people to higher productivity and quality. But as a businessman, I am required to lower down my moustache and work on the strength of others without being too critical and arrogant about their weaknesses. I have discovered the need for this unique blend of hard and soft attributes in my function.

A crisis of identity can create havoc on a human personality. The first victim of this is values. 'Shraddha' and 'gratitude' are two of the most synonymous and profound human values. They are not temporary phenomema of human life. When our identity is in crisis, we seem to lose these profound values and get attached to the small and inconsistent aspects like 'ahamkar' (ego) and pride. The pseudo personality of a man is born here.

There is often a conflict between my inner thoughts and my outer actions. I am driven by an urge to act, but I am held back from inside. There is a split and this upsets my tranquillity.

My thoughts are deeply influenced by my behaviour of the past — my conservativeness, prejudices and superstitions. I am so deeply influenced by them that, even today, I find myself greatly handicapped. I don't see any justice in being miserable this way. If one's life is not easily enjoyable every moment, then why should one live at all!

We are living for joy only. Apparently, there is no other meaning to our existence. Millions of us rub shoulders with each other every day, in and out, for the sake of ephemeral gains. There is so much of acrimony and unrest. Why? What are we going to sustain or attain?

Suddenly it strikes my mind that we are only working for a pure joy. The activities we are involved in seem to be less important than the joy they offer. We are all puppets in the hands of some unknown intelligence. Nobody knows what is its motive, but we are all revolving around its wisdom. Many activities which appear to be of major importance may bear very little meaning. But, our actions rendered with a spirit of joy are enough to impart much greater meaning and worth to our lives.

It is wiser to invest in people than in any other material or machine; and those people who invest in themselves happen to be the wisest.

Core values are of primary importance to an individual or an organisation. There is hardly any other identity for a man more than his own values. One who has not clearly ascertained his values is most vulnerable. Such people have a limited perspective and will always prove disloyal, selfish and unsympathetic to others in the long run. It is important for all employers to find out and guide their prospective employees to define their values before assigning jobs to them.

Whenever you see a person getting angry, restless or frustrated beyond proportion, you may conclude he is a victim of an identity crisis.

Identity is the common thread running through various activities of our life. Our values constitute the basic fibre of this thread. Whenever there is a crisis of such values, a crisis of identity is inevitable and vice versa.

I have seen many people who don't ascertain their values (first) before adopting an activity or assignment, they tend to acclaim the identity externally associated with such assignment as their own identity. This, in turn, tends to reflect their pseudo identity. They are, however, unable to sustain this identity permanently. They quit and blame their circumstances. They are impatient, restless and intolerant. They look for quick-fix justifications of their talents. When these do not happen, they go for an alternate career or business and look for other short-term fulfilments in their lives.

We don't attain anything, neither do we achieve or succeed. Every act of our life, effort or endeavour, is essentially a small act of self-actualisation. To realise this, every moment is a matter of great fulfilment and bliss.

What is the level and extent of one's awareness? This determines the nature, character and potential of a man. Every action of our life and every thought that precedes such action, affects our internal and external world. People with broader perspectives will bring about more far-reaching effects rather than their counterparts with narrower views, in spite of the fact that both of them are engaged in the same activity or endeavour.

In every decision, there is a chance to weigh between the loss and gain. And often, the 'loss and gain' have two perspectives. Decision making is more challenging due to clashes between these two perspectives. There is hardly any clash between the very loss and gain.

If there is a problem between two persons, neither party is right or wrong. There are two perspectives. The clash is based more on these two perspectives. So what do we do? We should help each other to explain the two perspectives from which we are to view the issue. We need to have an open mind to understand, assess and appreciate the mutual depth and broadness of the objectives and agree to accept the one that is based on the broader vision, encompassing the views of the two.

I never knew that even 'honesty' could be painful. There is a peculiar struggle between honesty to myself and honesty to others, and this seems to tear me apart.

On one hand, it is my commitment to someone I love, while on the other it is my passion. There is a third factor in the middle. It is my deep intention to be honest to myself. These three factors leave my mind bewildered and chaotic.

To know what are my own inner thoughts is so difficult. I am now sitting alone in my room. One hour has passed by, as if I have allowed this time to just fly away without knowing what has been actually happening inside me.

What is happening now? What am I thinking? Where is my mind right now? What are my discerning needs? What will make me happy? I just don't know...

I am in the midst of my past and present, i.e. in a state of nowhere. I am in a state of no 'identity'. I don't even know whether I am enjoying this state or not. I don't remember having been in a similar mental state ever before.

Prayer is the only way out. If all the doors around seem to be closed, then look up! The answer is beyond the bottom line. God has His unprecedented ways to bring solace to the tormented heart.

Life is like hide and seek. Is there anyone who is without any privacy? Is it possible to expose oneself completely to someone?

Imagine the number and type of thoughts that arise in our mind every moment. What transpires inside our mind, moment to moment? How much of it can we reveal? The question of action arises much later, but what about our thoughts ? How many times is it that our mind gets corrupted with naughty, uncivilised, disapproved thoughts? Why do we only blame wrong actions when we are unable to punish wrong thoughts?

Calmness brings divine energy unto us. It is just like osmosis. Inner calm creates concentration and vast sources of energy flow into the concentrated mind. Calmness cannot come until all negativities dissolve. Calmness is tantamount to purity and negativities are like sediments.

Regimentation is important. You begin by taking charge of yourself — your habits, body and mind. You come to respect yourself. You are blessed with a positive spirit always. This way your worries and tensions get mitigated.

Only intelligence has not made men successful. Intelligence along with guts generates success. Intelligence makes one calculative. Guts take the risk of imagination and open out new doors.

I am in the face of a challenge. Yet I can say, the best is happening now. There is productivity all the way — new discoveries and innovations. One needs time to think and remain calm and cool, and pray in silence. Pray, not beg, but to find new ways, gain confidence and strike relentlessly.

One's deepest emotions are significant aspects of one's character. At times, they cannot be concealed; but can completely predominate the mental state. I experience this very often, particularly when I hear old songs.

Ideas come and just keep flowing. There is an intoxication about such thoughts. They just go on and on. So colourful are they that you enjoy merely looking at them. One fine day you find these ideas uprooted from reality, i.e. cut away like a colourful kite.

There needs to be a creative discipline. These ideas need to be prioritised, sequenced and applied for action on 'first come first served basis'. Either the ideas are implemented or else, they tend to flow away.

I have been a consistent victim of creative indiscipline. This has brought me a lesser number of achievements than I have deserved.

It suddenly strikes as if sensitivity has something to do with emptiness. Emptiness not in a negative sense, for sensitivity is essentially a positive instinct! To be empty means to be eager. To be empty is to be qualified, potential and entitled, indeed. The sensitive mind is eager to attract and adapt to anything that seems to be around. To gain something, one has to first lose. Therefore, a teacher has to master the art of emptying the mind of the learner first.

My introspection revealed a unique new secret and it was again proved that a person's silent and deep awareness can only change him or her adequately, well before any formal acceptance or confession.

Long ago, I had launched a frenzied campaign of approval seeking (or importance hunting) at home. I blamed all and screamed at everyone and that too in the most obnoxious and aggressive manner. For, my own expectations from them were not fulfilled. My allegations were entirely based on my egocentric emotional demands, which at that point appeared most correct to me. Both the quantity and quality of my communication were unjust and sometimes untrue. What I did not care for at that stage was how my purer self or my higher intelligence witnessed this action of mine. I did not befriend my intelligence while I launched this massive campaign of self-importance and aggrandisement. My deeper intelligence, I know now, had consistently protested against such uncivilised behaviour of mine. I told it to 'shut up'. As my 'emotional me' went rampant on the surface, the 'intelligent me' was ready for a real showdown. This kind of encounter has been a consistently damaging factor in my life. Anger, like a fierce volcano, took the better of me. This only emanated from the skirmish between my two personalities. I disliked everyone and everything at home

Contd.

and I ran away to the outer world as an escapist, saying that I must attain everything that I had lost at home. If only I knew that my own anger at my apparent targets was my real enemy. I realised, though rather late, that my 'emotional self ' was not properly tuned to my 'intelligent self '.

We tend to divide ourselves due to our ever-unconscious journey to the peripheries. We are all at the peripheries, which is why we are distant from each other. The society, with all its efforts to modernise every moment, is taking us recurrently further from ourselves. Closest as we are to ourselves, we are equally closest to the Universe. At the centre we are one and at the peripheries we are different. To bring in inner harmony is to bring about absolute unison with the Universe. But unknowingly we are all dragging ourselves away. Isn't it something like being uprooted from the core? Our life is merely a journey outward from our centre. If only we knew how to stop and turn about, i.e. put the reverse gear. A journey towards our centre is a process of bringing about bliss in our lives.

People have energy. They want to do, but they need direction, a little respect and love. Once you give these, they will always be willing to die for a cause that is bona fide.

Until I have evolved from the levels of being only a son, brother, lover, servant or even a friend, I have not loved you, my God!

There is no departure, leaving or relinquishing; there is only reaching out to the impending new.

It is not necessary that the other man is right and you are wrong or vice versa when both fail to get along with each other. It is often true that the two parties are unable to click, despite the fact that there was nothing particularly wrong with either.

One's inner contentment that results from a sense of deep acceptance of one's actions and when such acceptance is not essentially the result of a rationalised analysis of those actions, then one becomes almost entitled to heaven.

Like all apparently bad encounters, the good things happening are also due to you. If you deserved the former, then even the latter was no less of an entitlement!

Take every trace of hatred out of my breath so that I can ever relinquish, when I have to, with love.

It never made any sense to me that spirituality needed to have a purpose. It need not have any priority over the physical or emotional states, expectations and aspirations. Spirituality need not exclude anything. It should rather include everything and then transcend all barriers. For, spirituality, in essence, is beyond every discrimination and definition.

If anything I wish to experience now offers a sense of 'compassion' that seems to be above all ephemeral expectations or apprehensions of having or losing, as the case may be, I become destined to meet such an experience soon enough.

I have keenly observed how my son plays. He talks on his own behalf and on behalf of the person with whom he interacts while playing simultaneously. I am astonished at his enthusiasm and absolute engrossment with the game he plays. He is lost in it completely and forgets all that is around him. He believes in all the objects and situations available for his game and these instantly, perhaps, come to occupy their places for him. He is without fear, apprehension, anxiety and worry. He is completely alert and perhaps is even beyond this state, all the while. I realise, indeed, a child is the guru from whom man can learn the best and the most.

The heaven's kindness has its own characteristic. When God gives, He does it so smoothly that you don't even feel His greatness. You feel, as if, you were entitled to it. Because God, unlike you, does not boast for the giving. This is why, most often, His blessings are not taken as His rewards. They come, appearing so casual. Only sometimes, and only to some people, it reveals that God only gave so much. At that moment, their eyes fill with tears, not only for the magnitude of His kindness but especially for the manner He gave, without even letting you know that He did.

When divinity descends on you and touches your thoughts and actions, these shape up in clear noble acts and become divine too.

It is not a matter of maximisation. It is rather actualisation of the mind's energy. For the mind itself has direct access to profound energy. In the normal course, the mind is adulterated by frequenting thoughts arising from our mundane activities. To render the mind free from these squandering thoughts is to concentrate the energy of the mind. One must first learn the mechanism of such evolving thoughts — how, wherefrom and why they come and then work through practical training, so that this unwanted wastage can be arrested. Through meditation we can partially contain and compose the mind, which is the reason that after meditation, we perceive great energy.

Often it appears that we have become thoughtless, but this is far from the truth. To be perfectly thoughtless is a difficult task. In fact, this is the ultimate pursuit of a 'yogi'. At our conscious level, we sometimes achieve the level of thoughtlessness. This in itself gives us plenty of joy. Imagine what absolute thoughtlessness will offer.

One way I learn is by putting my intelligence on the top and asking my mind to seek guidance from it. There are also those who advise you to surrender all your problems to God and let God solve them. There is a contradiction between the two apparently. For not surrendering problems to God itself can be due to utmost faith in Him that He will take care of you.

Life's greatest challenge is definitely not one in working out a relationship that is difficult, but in being forced to exist in one that has already failed.

The Indian education system of the ancient time was individualistic. The western education system on the other hand, has been institutional. The element of 'bhakti' however, has been common in both the sectors. In the east, 'bhakti' was a devotion to the guru while in the west, 'bhakti' was devotion to the work or to the purpose. Without 'bhakti', achievement and excellence are impossible.

In the west, educational schemes are drawn up through long and systematic research based on inputs gained from different sources, while in the east, the educational schemes are imparted by only one source which in turn constitutes a 'gharana.' In the east, the guru becomes an institution by himself.

I discovered that the guru is only an instrument to help a disciple recognise his own spiritual potential lying dormant within. Guru, indeed, gives nothing externally but only stimulates one's inner resources. The fine membrane that separates man from his own divinity is nothing but 'ego' or the 'I'. How then can ego be removed? 'I' is the refusal to bow down. So, 'to surrender' is the answer. How does one surrender? By way of 'bhakti' one does so. The solvent of 'bhakti' is so powerful that it dissolves ego effectively. How can one arouse this intensive 'bhakti'? The guru's personality can stimulate this spirit instantly!

* 'Bhakti' is a Sanskrit word which implies devotion, respect and submission, all in totality.

In one way, the Indian tradition is prominent and ahead. This is in the age of the conceptualisation of Shiva's dance. The symbol of Nataraj speaks everything of the cosmic dance of energies involved in the continually moving Universe. Dance is the core of the life cycle. The message that Indian dance conveys and the objective it carries is markedly and vastly different from that of any other country, especially the west. Dance in India was not evolved only to recreate the audience, but to communicate the latent truth that can help the audience transcend their smallness and achieve ecstasy, yoga or communion with the infinite.

There are two aspects of an art — the oriental and the occidental. Art, thus, is hardly complete with only one of these two facets. The orientals feel that their concept of art, which is based on contemplation and spiritualism, is higher than the occidental concept, which is based more on professionalism, or at best, external perfectionism. We must appreciate that days are changing. Today, art is not only a matter of private or individual choice of a handful of aspirants who would prefer to find their way through the woods, to reach a guru in the countryside to help them reach their cherished goals. There are any number of aspirants who are competent. Today, publicising art is not unethical. Occidental science plays its part in helping the art, not only in honing it physically, but in taking it far into the grassroots also.

People use divine powers for personal gains and then get frustrated. It stems from our typical rational thinking that 'seeing is believing'. We see the godly attributes to perform miracles and then get allured by the miraculous powers. We become a follower of this power, based on evidence of what we see, as if God is an object of test. Soon enough, when we don't get a positive result as it is natural to face failures in life, at least sometimes, we begin to lose faith. This is the time when life gets filled with regrets and mistrust of things. This is the time we lose faith in divinity. It is then that we find it difficult to return to divinity.

They search what is not anywhere. They search beyond themselves. This is like searching for the key outside in the streetlight because there is darkness inside. Searching is an effort that is always a waste. Contentment is in poise and vice versa. All things are in their respective places. Searching, therefore, is a mode of upsetting the order that is widely placed in the steady and secure hands of the infinite. To bring it within the temporary fold of the finite is only to cry later in despair. For, it is then lost; it would have passed away. Emptiness is the best order. It is perfectly akin to fulfilment. To search is to be nowhere — indeed, a fruitless, endless effort to reach the either pole. Cease to search and it is there. To cease is to let go in stillness and silence — without any skirmish, squandering or flickering. In silence, the eternal words spring; in mute, the divine music is manifested.

Our actions in general life emerge from thoughts. Can there be action without thoughts? If not, then will you say that the saints don't act? Actions can even flow from beyond the state of mind and such actions indeed are, perhaps, the purest form of actions. How can actions flow direct from the level of consciousness? First you go beyond the mind, which is in the realm of thoughts and is the store for memory. At the level of consciousness, it is a different atmosphere. Here you are not governed by thoughts, but by intuitions. You don't think; you act spontaneously. There is no conflict about what is right and what is wrong. What you do is proper, befitting your needs, perspectives and aspirations. Here you are at your best. You don't have to define your actions through the 'conscience' either. For, 'consciousness' is the very light of your soul which is above the mind; and conscience is perhaps just beneath the mind or is the spontaneous reflection of consciousness! When we say 'thoughts', we use the past tense. So, 'thoughts' in its true meaning cannot create any wonder in the present moment.

A mind full of 'thinking' is aware, alert and awakened. 'Thinking' is better for it is not a happening. It touches the wellspring of consciousness and produces some profound activity before becoming extinct. Soon, the next 'thinking' evolves. This is how the life's true beauty flowers and this is the 'tao' of living.

I have seen trust dwindling in the face of embarrassment. Was it real trust or was it an effort to bask in the glory of another person for a while? Was it merely an alternative to erstwhile frustration or a break from the monotony to freshen up, to nourish oneself with another's energy?

How can 'trust' break at the mild strike of the mundane world or due to an apparent fear of losing a social security?

Trust emanates from divinity and divinity cannot be an ephemeral perspective.

If there is one barrier between what we aspire for and what we achieve, it is most certainly the element of 'despair' mixed with our aspiration. Hope from which anxiety, haste and frustration are filtered off will entitle us only to those things we really need.

No science is an invention; it is merely a testimony or discovery within the premises of philosophy.

Am I attracted externally or driven from my core being? Is it an urge or euphoria? Or is it my inspiration? Do I need to insure, ensure or assure my faith, trust or support to someone? Or have I surrendered? Am I stimulated or influenced, or am I truly aroused or awakened? Will the feeling die down or lift me to an eternal life?

True friendship has a purpose. The purpose is also nobler than mere recreation, entertainment and soaking in each other's energy. Friendship has an element of illusion, so it tends to sway one away from the macro perspective or project. When friendship supersedes the purpose, then it can strike a cruel blow even to the innocent. It also tramples over a few other important relations like parents, teachers and other compassionate companions. In such deluded moments, in the apparent sway of glory, one unconsciously ignores a massive umbrella that has been covering him all the while. He does realise the realities soon, but often not sooner, when it gets too late.

Amidst all physical uncertainties, how I steadily flow! My prayers hold me up. There is not even an iota of fear at that moment. I never thought that my job market would be so awfully low. Rather, I had always thought that getting a job would be quite easy for me. Everyone has a job, but I haven't got one. What hard work I have put in, how much money I have spent in making my biodata and applications, how many doors I have knocked on. I have literally left no stone unturned, but I have been turned down by my fate. Normally this would make one completely frustrated and perhaps, mad. I have a lot of responsibility: I am the father of two growing children who have no one else to look upto. Yet, I have a deep confidence in my bosom that this will pass and I will not perish.

The human mind is indeed a paradox. We make promises and give gifts to announce our faith and trust. We are eager to prove our sincerity to the other person by singing, writing, speaking, dining and doing many more extraordinary things. We count days for someone's arrival, we take leaves for sharing dreams and our glorious pasts and achievements.

What an irony, we take a minute to shatter all the trust, promise and goodwill in a momentary thrust of wind that seems to threaten our own status, personal vanity or security.

We are prepared to forsake the price of time to build the trust, but deny the price of tolerance to sustain it through crises.

I need to look rather deeply at my own response to someone's concern for me. For all miseries of life are only the results of lack of concern from a friend, a fellow-man, a neighbour or a lover. Then how can concern be bad or be negative or disturbing? When one's genuine concern disturbs me, it is most likely that I am plagued by age-old conventions, fears, apprehensions and preconceived notions in my assessment of that very concern. If there was nothing between me and someone's genuine concern for me, it could change my response phenomenon. My own response to others' concern needs to change. If only I could react with a positive response, my life would undergo a complete transformation.

It suddenly struck me deeply the other day that we need to learn a lot from people who have less material assets and status than us in the society. The ones whom we use for serving our comforts and material needs are those who have to work in our households to keep us going in the society. We preach attitude to people, we talk about our help and contribution to the downtrodden in our society. We believe, and we perhaps do know a great deal, at least more than those who are not so educated and academically qualified as us. However, we do often fall short of working out life's problems than them in the world.

'Questioning' is a matter of attitude. It comes out of a humble effort to learn. It is a quest for growth and self-actualisation, and it is most welcome.

The rest of it is justification, or at best clarification. Some people develop opinions based on their own strength or weakness. It is an idea that suits their mechanism. They do not have any conviction; what they have is bias. Then they ask and in that asking there is a discreet motive of justifying their own viewpoint. If it is an unconscious effort to testify or seek an endorsement of one's own point of view; it is not true 'questioning'.

My mind is steadily learning to be in the present. A sense of transparency tends to prevail between me and my surroundings, like the trees in the autumn, the tender breeze that blows through their pale yellow leaves and the typical fragrance that it carries right into my soul. It is as if all these have a direct contact with me and there is nothing in between — no image, no barrier. And this brings in a smooth and consistent feeling of joy that spontaneously tends to linger for a long time. There is no difference between me and my joy — the me that sees and the object that is seen, both mingle into a unique abstractness. Suddenly, I find myself relieved from my past and this spontaneity also supersedes a tangible purpose which my mind would otherwise explore. It is a unique state of meditation that seems to lift me into abundance.

Happiness in a marriage is possible. A clear perspective on its limitations is a prerequisite. This perspective in itself needs to be positive. On one hand, this perspective should essentially have more than spiritual, its social and intellectual dimensions, while on the other, because it is less spiritual, its very importance need not be under-toned or abandoned. For, the illusion of life is as important as is the need to transcend its domain.

Love for God is not affection, respect, passion, loyalty or anything of the sort. It is different, in so far as it encompasses all these forms of love to bring forth a new kind of intensity that can only be experienced.

My inability to forgive is the cause of all my sufferings. If only I could just let go. If only I could say once, 'Okay, alright, I have got whatever and howsoever I should have, and now I have no malice, towards anyone; this place is big enough for all of us', then all my problems would be over. I still long for this cherished breakthrough.

If your mind is filled with a blissful serenity, a positive thought every moment, then you will definitely feel like being on the right track, anticipating great things to happen on the way. This strengthens you more, and you will soon be linked to your higher consciousness. You will attain profound patience, remain cheerful and your mind will be alert to meet the right opportunity.

The naked truth is that nature loves to embrace you without everything that you seem to own.

The actions of an enlightened person can be apparently confusing. This is because of the tendency of man to judge all things and beings on the basis of his own perception formed in the life passed. Such a judgement or opinion is often cynically conditioned. A simpler way to go about it is to find out if the person in question has genuine higher values to preach and practice. Let this be the deciding factor to consider the person as a friend or a mentor, rather than being unduly confused, alarmed, or upset.

Who, under the sun, has the guts to say, 'I am leaving it all behind'? All things and beings are precious possessions of an infinite energy which alone pervades them all. Things which come our way are blessed aspects of that divinity and to think of discarding any one of them is like shunning divinity itself. Life, of course, is a journey that requires travelling from one place to another and as such, one needs to go for the impending new as a matter of response to life's call. What may appear to have been left behind in the process is something one never possessed at all.

An experience that soothes the soul and brings you out of a trauma, and if you can perceive its warmth with deep contentment and bliss, as if it was a gift from heaven, then this very experience will be essentially divine, in spite of others' judgments to the contrary.

There are moments when the heart speaks without any sound that is externally audible and in that speech, some great things are heard which can't be retold even to self, much less to anybody else.

I want to 'be', but not 'have'. For, frequently hanging between 'having' and 'not having' is most painful.

I could clearly perceive the breeze blowing through the large window of the National Library and bringing in pure fragrance of the autumn. The cuckoo sang from one of the large trees and which I could hear while reading on my desk. I loved this majestic library and everything about the atmosphere. My heart danced with pure joy and exhilaration!

Love transcends all smallness in this life, leaving behind all fears, apprehensions, worries and expectations. This life will become memorable when I shall rise to that level from where I can experience this feeling.

Some societies, countries and religions have set forth their own sets of moral codes to monitor as to who is good and who is bad. It is so much in their blood that they get surprised when they meet or interact with another set of people who have apparently different or no such stipulated codes. In fact, there are people who operate at a higher mental level where the aspect of external moral codes becomes least relevant. These are the people who are endowed with higher virtues and stronger mental energy. These people synthesize their mental resources through greater creativity, while the standard practitioners of the so-called codes are a sort of analysts, who are rather busy in merely perfecting their mundane way of life.

Whenever I operate through my consciousness, all barriers between me and my surroundings immediately vanish and I plunge into a kind of joy that takes me beyond all fear, hatred and shame. My life starts swinging and beaming with ecstasy, that sweeps everything around me back into my consciousness itself.

The truth lies between the finite and the infinite. Man performs his tasks within the limited framework of moral codes. He has to comply with the social norms and their dictates. He can't supersede, neither can he run away. Rather, he has to accept all that is asked for with an utmost sense of commitment. But how can he salvage himself? How can he reach the core of his soul, which is by far his only goal? He has to find freedom amidst the limits of his duty. Depending on the intensity of his urge, sincerity of quest and his own basic nature, he will certainly find his way to freedom. He will transcend all the barriers and his destiny will bring him to the threshold of truth and so he will go alone. Not even the call of age-old convention, tradition or any other shallow barrier or pseudo ethics can hold him back.

If you want to change your past, the only way is to attend to your present with your utmost best because this present moment is about to become your past tomorrow. With intense goodness for the present, you deliver positive memories into your past, that can effectively neutralise the erstwhile negative accumulations in your store.

Discipline is not a matter of physical application or external adaptation of certain dictated codes and modes. It is essentially a self-motivated set of principles that needs to become an integral part of our character and should therefore encompass all walks of our life.

Whenever you have a conflict with another person, or are asked to mediate in the one taking place between two persons, just be at the centre, and never be on any side or even be away. Truth is never on one side of an apparent conflict between two opposites. Truth exists between the opposites. In fact, it hides deep in their centre. You cannot identify it; rather, you have to be in it. Not only the world, even the Universe shows a beautiful balance, with everything being in a wonderful harmony. No balance is ever drawn between two alikes; rather, this is a result of two opposites that neutralise each other — the plus and the minus; the darkness and light; the male and the female; the last and the first. No part is complete without the other. Being on one side signifies only incompleteness, a kind of inadequacy, an immaturity! All things are good enough in their respective places. Peace means a deep, subtle sense of fulfilment within a feeling that consistently tells me that I am alright, I am okay, all things are right in their places; they don't disturb me at all. I work only because I have to and I have no need, no competence to set anything right. I am neutral within myself. I just respond to something that moves me from above and I give myself unto that call, totally and unconditionally. I have no need for any judgement or decision.

To follow certain moral codes, dictated by whoever it be, is not in the best order. Rather, it is possible to really train the mind to go over all the apparently specified codes. By means of such a training one can learn to contain and compose one's emotions and even to maximise one's mental energy, so that one can, indeed, walk over the so-called sets of right and wrong. This way one would reach a stage of 'beyond ethics'. After all, codes bear an objective; so, codes are the only apparent means, not the end. A trained mind is spontaneously objective, so, it is impossible for it to be unethical.

I wonder why my own convention interferes with my freedom! More than the sense of duty, it is something else that always tends to pull me back, despite the fact that I know there is nothing there. Knowing that it is hell, I just continue to exist in it. This is life's greatest irony. People, society and the convention (of my own bringing up) always tend to disturb my peace and discreetly threaten me of some kind of an unpleasant consequence. In apprehension of this unseen consequence and without the knowledge of its gravity, I choose my present misery, almost accepting it as inevitable. Even acceptance of the present misery is devoid of any contentment due to my conviction that amongst the past, the present and the future, it is only the present that lies within my control.

Life presents itself in a new manner every moment. Being in this newness, every moment becomes the 'tao'. Apparently, I am passing through some hard moments now. But, the most delightful part is that I have started realising that this period will pass. All miseries lie in the apprehension of a possible conclusion or end. When I know that I am on an endless journey that includes miseries, worries and even death, only then do I discover the real ecstasy or 'tao' of life.

It suddenly strikes that disloyalty or loyalty is not the point though this very often appears to be the bone of contention. There is something prior to this. If at all there is disloyalty or mistrust, there must have been some absence of love. If there is love, then there is forgiveness, for the inability to forgive is a consequence of the inability to love. Forgiveness is tantamount to acceptance, and if there is acceptance, then there is no conflict. So, before I go on to blame someone for his action, I must first check if I have primarily failed with the person at some basic level. And on the other hand, if I am inclined to act disloyally, let me be sure that I have failed in some basic quarter and I am taking this derogatory action as a compensatory response of my failure. What is more important is a deep awareness of my wrong which will help to change my action for the better.

Intolerance and irritation do not seem to leave me. I am still deeply affected by my situations and the people around me. I get worked up. Why? I know some of my people are not efficient and there have been frequent embarrassments and losses in business, but, why can't I get down to working out specific strategies that will help me attain better results from my surroundings, rather than getting wild and mad so often?

'Will' is different from 'desire'. In the track of our growth sometimes we get confused about how to attain or achieve things in life without 'desire'. It appears that it is just impossible to get anywhere without the 'will' to be there. The 'will' or 'intention' is rudimentary. The wisdom lies here; the 'will' is open-ended. The sole pursuit that is latent in a 'will' is pure joy. On the other hand, there is always an element of attachment linked to every 'desire'. One needs to deeply contemplate on these two words: 'will' and 'desire'. 'I will to' is an absolutely different concept than 'I desire to'. 'Will' is free and victorious; 'desire', on the contrary, has already victimised or affected you somehow, to some extent! 'Desire' can bring some catastrophe one day while 'will' has the potential to grow into a never-ending ecstasy. To transform our 'desire' into 'will' is, by far, the greatest challenge to mankind. 'Will' is a spiritual aspect. All religious scriptures, in essence, have invited mankind to draw this profound line of demarcation between 'will' and 'desire'.

Nature provides everything to the deserving. There is no more available to man than what he deserves. The tormented soil deserves raindrops. The blossomed flower emits fragrance and then attracts the bees. Man evolves to a higher level and fortune gravitates unto him.

Aim signifies direction and goals the milestones. Both are essential aspects of life's journey. One pulls you towards the destination and the other keeps pushing you further on the track. Together, they create the needed momentum for you to flow towards your destination.

The apparent space we seem to create between us and our surroundings is often not the one which denotes the actual distance. Only time can say if at all there was a distance or not!

Aspiration is necessary. It kick starts you to action. Achievements too are rather important, for they help you to sustain your actions till the time you reach the highway of life. Now, the preparatory part is over and the real journey begins. Harder the preparation, smoother is the journey.

I must take revenge, why not? I am not dead and passive — a spiritless weakling! Forgiveness? I don't believe in forgiveness without action. 'God will punish' or 'nature will take its course — such expressions cut little ice with me. I know even God won't forgive me, if I don't do my part. My religion itself had her birthplace in the battle field. So, I for one, shall not let my adversaries go without a fight. Fighting in my dignity, my honour, my respect for life and above all my faith in God.

I am, of course, angry; but I am not too blind to see my anger as a gift. I shall use it to bring victories for myself, yet not become its victim. My fury is, therefore, full, firm and free to fall only upon my adversaries. My war is on! Live or die, I aim to win....

The whole world is craving! People are hungry. Hungry not so much for their physical food, but more for everything else. This is a rat race! All are running — no matter where and for what! Just running! Will they attain? Will they reach somewhere?

It is a hunger. And the character of hunger is to feel hungry again and again and, therefore, remain hungry forever. Think of hunger: it has a wide mouth. It is forever open, as if there is no end to its appetite.

Achievement and success in their true forms are never a product of hunger. By being hungry you don't achieve anything. For, hunger and peace are parallel lines. To perform great feats, happiness is a must. It is simply an imperative. By being happy, you can apply your maximum endeavour to your work. When you are happy, you have a steady flow of energy. You can concentrate more. Only then can you evolve from hunger and realise a spiritual life.

Eklavya offered his thumb and was abandoned by his guru Dronacharya. He left in silent dignity, without protest. Was he weak or was he rich enough in his faith and reverence? He prayed in solitude and nothing ever disturbed his faith and gratitude.

Please accept this birthday wish, gratitude and regard from someone in exile. My name is not important; but rest assured, I shall carry your flag and carry out your mission. I have completed my course because I have actually seen the best and the worst and now I seem to be actually beyond it all.

With love and prayers...

Love is the most generous of all attributes. It sacrifices and gives way. It toils, pays its price and plays its part. It stays ahead of others and when the call comes, smilingly it inspires one to donate blood, kidney or eye. It is modest like a tree, tender like petals and sensitive like a pregnant mother. It travels down the beaten track to reach its beloved in pain.

Love is also majestic like a monarch, dignified like a saint and bright like sunshine. It rises above every gloom of doubt and stays above board in abiding glory. It is far away from pity; as for sympathy, no, never — it will suffocate in disrespect, starve in neglect and die in indifference.

Love will forever adjust, but will hardly compromise, just as the king will prefer death than to accept prison. Love will forever respond in need, but will never act in redundance.

Thank you, God, for this thought that comes in the course of severe pain.

Privacy is a way of life. One is justified in having it. Our social systems are built over this legitimate allowance. But secrecy is another thing. This is an external action based on internal fear, prejudice or superstition. It does not reflect courage, confidence or conviction.

Values and principles are not aspects of lip service. They are the results of a subtle and deep self-realisation. They are not only externally acquired but are internally crystallised through silent contemplation. Rather than being loudly pronounced, they glaringly manifest themselves through the way we live our lives.

If someone appreciates you, just accept the joy and pass on the pride to your Creator. Both the joy and appreciation will then be sustained for life.

A central purpose is important. This holds everything together. When there is no purpose in life, then life falls apart, just like a house of cards. Even relaxation needs to have a discerned purpose. An unplanned holiday becomes a boring experience often. The purpose happens to be the sole integrating factor that harmonises the various functions of life. Life becomes interesting and meaningful by the sheer dint of a purpose.

We live our life with a shallow context. The context is the most important aspect. The other name for context could be perspective. The narrow perspective of life is to revolve around the realm of 'I'. All our attitudes and vision consequently assume a narrow shape and we dwindle in confusion. There are only some rare men who have achieved a larger or broader perspective or have transcended the narrow domain of existence and attained a higher quality of life. They have lived above all conflicts, inequalities and confusions. Their lives are stabilised on the basis of firm conviction.

Do we have a difference? Is it something that we can't even talk? Let us not talk, touch or do anything of the like. Instead, let us walk under this vast blue sky. Let us unite, not with patience, but with faith. Our thoughts for each other will cause our footprints to meet somewhere, some day.

There is always a kind of struggle waging inside me. This is a positive state of affairs. In fact, this struggle actually defines my inner core nature. The moment I realised this fact, I had an enlightening experience. I was filled with a deep sense of relaxation, as if I had learnt to accept myself — this new identity of mine.

There have been ephemeral moments of depression in my life, when I found that I did not live upto the standards I had set for myself or when I preached to my folks. I was almost ready to embalm myself with failure. That was the moment I realised that I was missing the most important fact. I was yet struggling to come up despite the fact that I was not up to the mark.

My mind was filled with forgiveness and I could happily define myself as a person of continuous inner struggle in order to become nicer, better and more enlightened than what I was in the past.

Possibility means extension of the mental threshold. Every achievement is a possibility that exists within the thinking power of the mind. With regular practice one can augment this threshold and thereby become entitled to greater accomplishments.

Joy that spontaneously results from a bonafide activity is a divine gift. Let it be accepted with open arms and shared only with the divine. This joy is different from the joy that one expects, for the expected joy is hardly sustained and is rather likely to bring misery as an aftermath. The joy that flows as an unexpected reward is the sole inspiration and blessing for man.

King Dasarath thought that Ram would sit on the throne of Ayodhya; Kaikeyi thought Bharat would be the king; but Bharat wanted the 'paduka' to be on the throne.

Bharat is the greatest character in the epic Ramayana. Bharat ruled the kingdom, sitting on the floor and represented the 'paduka', which was symbolic of supreme justice or God's wish. This way our own thoughts when surrendered to God's thought tend to get baptised.

We are no kings. We are actually the gatekeepers of the king's throne. The king is actually an honour — the supreme responsibility. As a king, our task is to ensure that the supremacy and honour of 'dharma', truth and justice are maintained.

One, who has shifted himself from his core belief, aim and vision, becomes an eternal victim of an identity crisis. In spite of all his wealth and luxury, he is hollow, like an empty metallic drum. He is so confused that he doesn't even know where he stands. He identifies himself with certain pseudo external identity and ends up becoming arrogant towards others. Inside, he suffers consistently.

In every sphere of life, I have come across a number of otherwise potential individuals being ruined thus.

Let me learn to approve my external actions internally at every moment. A spontaneous internal sanction to any external action is the greatest challenge.

I have realised that a 'sin' takes place much before an action. The action without the internal sanction tends to become a sin. Any activity that is devoid of internal sanction has in itself the intrinsic misery. You don't have to even wait for its aftermath, or what you would call reaction. It is there, right at that moment. Check how much of your actions receive your internal sanctions.

Why don't I sanction all my actions? Am I not free? Am I victimised, immobilised or imprisoned? When I am inspired to act on something, it is my spontaneity. So where is the problem? Let me expand my internal allowances and discover the joy of an abundant life! Isn't freedom itself free from even an iota of fear or evil?

I shall become enlightened when I am able to distinguish between aspects that personally hurt me from those threats that affect the cause of others who are the ultimate beneficiaries of my work.

Quite often there is a clash between how a situation affects me personally vis-à-vis how it affects the macro cause. When I learn to look up to the macro purpose above my own joy and frustration, only then do I become truly entitled to lead a movement to a meaningful end.

This attitude seems to be the true spirit of all achievers in life.

All languages first reach the intelligence. Some of them are striking enough to arrive at the doorway of the heart. Most don't; so they are stored as memories.

Music is a different kind of language and perhaps, the only one that transcends the barrier of intelligence to strike right at the door of the heart. It, therefore, enchants and overwhelms the soul completely.

We present 'courtesy' in the form of 'gratitude'. These are two different aspects; in that, 'gratitude' has a much deeper connotation. Anyone can be courteous, but gratitude is a matter of 'character'. It comes from within. It has to be developed through toil, penance and deep contemplation.

Courtesy is nice for it is good behaviour, but to develop 'shraddha' one requires to undergo a transformation of one's deep inner core.

*Shraddha is a Sanskrit word encompessing love, respect, gratitude and obedience, all at once.

We only resist our needs and wants. Every small frustration, failure and rejection impedes our path to self-fulfilment. These impediments are only our feelings. We need to purify our feelings. Our consciousness is the touchstone. If we remain in contact with our consciousness, every time we feel, then our feeling will be pure. This purity is divine. It will bring in a divine order in our lives and we shall come to receive everything that we need or want.

There is a space between seeing or hearing and feeling. Often this space tends to be inside. You can also call this space a 'gap'. Our thoughts, which are essentially influenced by our past experiences, await this gap. The moment there is a gap, such thoughts will enter and contaminate our feelings. Meditation is all about reducing this space or gap. Meditation refers to merely experiencing of the feeling without prior thought or judgement.

Who can fight except the one who is strong? I am a fighter. Fighting is in my spirit; it is my core nature. I can stand up and protest against an injustice. I don't want to let someone go without fighting. I am not a hypocrite. I don't pretend to forgive when I lack the courage and strength to do so.

Non-violence is not the expression of a weakling.

Too much planning and less of action have immobilised me. There is very little meaningful output. A lot of time is spent on finding a new method in order to cope with the challenges of life, but most of the time I find that we haven't begun acting or working on the solution.

I want to live a pure life; the life that is most respectful to me. I have realised how painful it is to have people's respect but simultaneously fail to live upto one's own expectations. One gets just torn apart.

People blame others more out of their inner pains than anything else. Consequently, they also define themselves by such acts more than by defining others. Inner frustrations reflect in the form of a vendetta, which splits one's personality even more, agonising the person from within. His vision gets disrupted and he is unable to see things in the right perspective.

I have seen that people's frustrations often emanate from their inability to accept a situation the way it comes in their life. Most of them can neither accept it nor agree within themselves to own their legitimate responsibility. It is a kind of escapism which ultimately prompts the person to pass the whole blame on to the other man.

This creates a divisible atmosphere, full of misunderstandings. Unfortunately, this is likely to cause more loneliness and skirmishes within the person. It may result in cynicism and make the victim play deceptive games of doubtful standards in the outer world.

If a man is able to comprehend the problems of such a person and when there is no other apparent means to help the person, he should at least pray for the welfare of this person.

Prayers do work, believe me.

When I have a deep inner calm, I seem to discover a deeper purpose to life than the one that is seemingly visible on the surface.

The subtle mind can only sense this subtle existence of a deep purpose. We need to extend this subtle state of our mind in order to render it more and more alert and sensitive.

When we are able to integrate the externally incomprehensible episodes to apprehend, perceive and describe the much broader and more divine spiritual purpose, only then we learn the real 'Art of Living'. Then our so-called mundane existence transcends into a life of higher order and life itself becomes a song, dance, music, poetry or a sculpture.

Of late my own thoughts have become steadier than ever before. As I have learnt to slow down my external pace, my mind seems to have become more dynamic, consistent and clear. I have discovered more faith, joy and confidence in all activities.

I wonder why I took so much time to realise this new way of living. I am confident now that this is a happier, steadier and a more successful way to life.

Being alone is so gloriously beautiful. You find that you have lost everything that was originally not yours! Now you are alone!

You are now left with nothing that you acquired on the track. Now you will be no longer busy in doing anything with those that are lost.

You are now with yourself, all alone. There is enough time to deal with yourself. For, you are the most precious gift to yourself and you now have this exclusive gift and nothing else. Will you now start digging, delving within, to discover everything that was, if at all, ever more precious and meaningful?

The joy of being entitled and deserved is by far the most divine experience. There are two ways for people to receive recognition. Most receive them in the form of their own success, while some receive them as blessings. The latter sustain more.

We need to ask ourselves before we attempt to offer our sympathy or concern for another individual, 'Am I prepared to take the genuine responsibility of the individual for his or her pain?' If we get a 'yes' answer from our bosom, then our concern is truly benevolent. Otherwise, it would be deemed as curiosity rather than concern. Curiosity, contrary to genuine concern, is a disentitled interference in other's business. Hence, this is vulgar and uncivilised.
If we think carefully, we will see that it is always better to pray for another person rather than to come forward to offer any uncalled for sympathy.

We, human beings, are sometimes stranger than we appear. We are more curious about personal and private matters of others. Even the possibility of a scandal excites us beyond proportion. We become extraordinarily active and enthusiastic to dig out facts and information. Our creative mind is then in full cry. We make the issue more juicy and spicy. Then we sit down and relish the item with like-minded people. It is our unconscious way of proving our own innocence, worth and importance to ourselves.

We try to portray such curiosity by showing our willingness to help, by sympathising, or showing concern for the other person. Interestingly, many of us who do this are highly qualified and hold key positions. What is most ironical is that this entire process has become so ingrained in our minds that we ourselves are consciously unaware of our own manipulations.

Will a positive mind spend time and energy to deplore others or will it develop oneself in order to attain one's self-worth and esteem? Only the lazy ones amongst us become so perverted, malicious and deceptive.

What is the consequence? We build a pseudo world of self-importance and continue to live there as a neurotic for the rest of our lives. This brings miseries at the end of the day, as our conscience, which is a witness to our true motive, will not spare from pricking us.

I must wait, for, if I don't, I lack faith in the heaven's treasures due to me. To hurry is to be greedy like a dog, and so, I must bear with patience. And what do I have to lose, if I was entitled to love, or if I had indeed risen above all my smallness? Love itself is a reward and there is no reward for love. I should be fortunate if I am discovered for and by love. And why am I rushing for gaining more? As my sanctity, pureness and patience have brought me rewards in the form of being able to love, have I not already become blessed? And nothing more should I want except to float in its ecstasy and abundance, for only with more faith and trust in it can I discover its greater depth and intensity.

I don't have to possess what I love. I just need to click with it. It should only tell me that it has been waiting for me. It is not just unknown, but as if known to me infinitely. When it came, I knew it was coming and that was it. And, there was no beginning to it and no end. Perhaps, it has by character no past, no future.

Is honesty a matter of assessment based on certain apparent action or is it beyond assessment at all? I want to be always honest and I am sure that I harbour no more prevailing thought that is not bona fide. Yet, I am often unable to act on the basis of such thoughts. When I consider the atmosphere around me to hold my sincere thoughts deep inside, then do I become an escapist, or am I then a victim of fear? I suffer from conflict between the urge for absolute freedom and my having to consider my environment for wherever it belongs.

I deprived someone of her purity by making her a part of the social structure. I have unknowingly made her an object of an experiment that seems to draw a painful inference that 'I have almost lost her'. She was a woman when I loved her. My love died when I made her my wife. I did not know that the wife is a condition; or, better still, by the word 'wife' I have failed to understand the meaning beyond the set of social responsibilities and commitments that is vested in this terminology. I have curbed her freedom and, this way, I have compromised mine too. Our lives are lost now amidst a peculiar jugglery of destiny where both of us move continuously as parallels. The fact that we can't do without each other, as we are complementary in the juggle, appears to be the greatest of all ironies.

My inner thoughts seem to flow alone most indifferently. How much about these do I understand and perceive on the surface of my mind? My thoughts, on the surface, wander rootlessly and make me feel fatigued often, like a departed kite. They have their extended hands stretched inside at the inner thoughts, but still helplessly flow away. The inner thoughts serenely look at them from the windows of my heart, unable to reach out and embrace them. How long will I continue to be torn away between my thoughts?

Some of my crucial rights lie beyond myself. And I often act on my rights without, effectively, owning their custody. Life, as such, is reduced to an effort of having to attain the legitimacy of making the true beginning of itself. For, action without a possessed right, tends to become a social liability. At times, however, I land up discovering my possession of such an authority; yet, to my dismay, I realise soon that I had actually flicked it away while the world momentarily closed its eyes. And I did not know my resultant status, till I did this many times. Now, life has become a wit-game of mutual alertness between my external world and myself. I am left to play patience by compulsion while I would love to go for one of my choices.

She came triumphantly, unobservantly. The birds chirped. The beaming morning sunlight smiled on the lush green lawn of the library. The old trees in their wise silence sang her glory deep into my soul. The books on my reading table read notes on her introduction…All these together told me, in earnest, that I was indeed waiting for her arrival with all my heart and soul. I touched her in tenderness and my lips trembled...and I could only murmur, 'Be there, where I am.'

How to determine the ethics of an action has been my quest. In the matter of ethics, I always find myself externally dependent. But, between considering ethics of an action externally and not considering it at all, the latter almost always seemed more comfortable. The moment I arrived at this conclusion, I needed to inquire if ethics were rather an internal feature. For, it seems as if ethics tend to adhere to the so-called external conditions and that proved to be a myth. The point becomes pertinent because in spite of being externally threatened, my actions have positive joy for those who are directly concerned with them. The attached predicament, tension and worry, however, are generally the aftermaths and are related less to the internal spirit of the act. What remains to be an irony is that I still have to look out for my freedom externally.

The girl's name is Shibani. She helps us look after our household as both my wife and I work outside. She cooks, she bathes our son, loyally maintains our property, cleans our clothes and utensils, mops the floor and what not. Without her we are undone. That day she came under the scorching sun, just a little late than usual. The delay in her arrival upset us immensely as we had come to depend on her. My daughter jokingly remarked, 'Shibani Didi, you are late!' It struck a discordant note right then and I promptly reprimanded my daughter softly. We were having the afternoon lunch at that point. I told my wife, 'Let us imagine for a while that you or I had to do the work which she will begin doing now. All this work is only for others' benefit. Cooking and cleaning are only to serve others' needs. Imagine, if we had to do it almost in the same manner as we had to cook and clean our own home...(perhaps a little better!). After the work we would go home (while our employers would have the afternoon rest), take our bath and feed our son then. And you would have to hurry because soon you would have to report back for the evening chores.'

Shibani lovingly replied back to my daughter, 'Why are you so upset, my dear?' as she went into the kitchen. I looked at her in complete indebtedness and said to myself, 'You teach me life.' If I were you I would hate the people who make me do this work.

Contd.

Memory is a highly reliable 'unrealiable factor'. It can be easily washed off the surface of the mind. What seems to be the most important aspect of today, and what you think is going to remain, can even pass away when you become accustomed to being without it long enough. The memory is never more loyal to an event than excitement. It would, therefore, accept an event of greater excitement and conveniently relinquish another, which is held so far, of lesser intensity. The paradoxical why of the mind is exploited by all publicity and advertising agencies to capture mass attention. In fact, one is called smarter when one knows how to benefit from this vulnerability of the human mind. On the contrary, lack of knowledge and experience this phenomenon have caused hopelessness, depression and sufferings for many. Even betrayals, for that mater, may not always mean a conscious action by someone to victimise another, for it could well be a treachery of the memory to own up a more impulsive idea at the cost of an old one.

As life has both aspects—joys and sorrows—no learning is ever complete only with good examples, teachings and events. In fact, one learns more by facing the hard times. In spite of experiencing my due share of anger, malice and vengeance, when I was suddenly left alone by a host of people upon whom I had counted the most, I could make myself rise above such feelings. When I now look back to those hours of trials and tribulations, my heart fills with gratitude for all those who left me and made me learn to face life all by myself.

And there are many more whom I cannot list but who have contributed in no small measure to my experience.

Do you love a 'part' or 'the whole'? Remember love is ' the whole'. 'The whole cannot love a 'part'. 'The whole' would only mingle into 'the whole'. This is Nature's law. So, if they don't mingle, be sure, they were essentially not 'wholes' – they were 'part' versus 'part' or 'part' versus 'the whole'. 'The whole' would have had some of its parts as 'good or noble' while some others as 'bad or evil'; but now they are all dissolved into 'the pure whole'.

The 'pure' is above board and in that it was even above 'good or noble'. This is why love is essentially pure and calling it 'good or noble' will only render its definition far from 'the whole'

I can't, therefore, love the good things in you. I can only love you.

That I cannot ever be unselfish is one of my most serene realisations of life. I, indeed, wonder if anyone could be truly unselfish. It is, however, quite ironical that one's level of self-actualisation is only proportionate to the extent one is actually unselfish. Knowing this, I have unconsciously shifted my struggle to finding out the actual extent of my own selfishness and unselfishness from my erstwhile efforts to be unselfish. This process of self-analysis has evidently placed me on a faster track of self-realisation.

I would blame my fate and destiny and say in utter despair, 'Am I not a human being; am I not entitled to look after my own child and give him due company? Do I not deserve more sympathy and love of the society?' I told myself, 'You are great in every way: you smile politely, you love my children, you are indebted to us for nothing, you don't bear any hatred in your heart, you serve with pleasure, you don't care for your own health and you work hard for a few chips, which certainly are far from enough to buy you even the minimum of pleasures or satisfaction.' Instantly I discovered the truth about happiness and I felt very small in front of this young girl.

My privileged pride did not allow me to express my feelings, but all my love for this girl poured out and I said to myself, 'You don't deserve any sympathy, for, you are much enriched and happy. If there was a God, He must be with you, much before I could lay a claim to His blessings.'

'Honesty' is a matter of character, but 'frankness' is one of behaviour. Both have their supreme places in their respective guarters. Each, as a masterpiece can independently exalt a person's profile. Honesty will create a powerful history for a man while frankness will let him expand his geographical boundaries on Earth. The former refers to foundation and the latter to architecture. Honesty establishes the repute of a man, while frankness helps him to build his world by creating a bond of trust. These two aspects bear both integral and independent features of a man's personality. One without the other has the power to separate him from the crowd, but when present together, they would make him stand the test of time and space. Frankness needs to be rooted in honesty. Honesty, on the other hand, should cherish its existence by manifesting its fragrance through frankness.

How to determine the ethics of an action has been my quest. In the matter of ethics, I always find myself externally dependent. But, between considering ethics of an action externally and not considering it at all, the latter almost always seemed more comfortable. The moment I arrived at this conclusion, I needed to inquire if ethics were rather an internal feature. For, it seems as if ethics tend to adhere to the so-called external conditions and that proved to be a myth. The point becomes pertinent because in spite of being externally threatened, my actions have positive joy for those who are directly concerned with them. The attached predicament, tension and worry, however, are generally the aftermaths and are related less to the internal spirit of the act. What remains to be an irony is that I still have to look out for my freedom externally.

Every life has a central story with a definite moral or maxim. It is true that only a negligible few among the whole human race read, much less understand, their own stories and the morals thereof. But those who are able to do this not only make their own life meaningful, but leave an inspiration for others to follow. This story tends to describe the very identity of life. It is unfortunate that most lives continue to get lost in the deep and dense forest of this world without leaving any footmark; but those who do unwittingly chart out their own maps tend to define their distinguished territories or identities.

Those who accumulate pains and sufferings, though called oversensitive, are often misunderstood by the rest. Generally appearing to be desolate, indifferent and lonely, they endure the suspicion or comments of their folks as if they were too subservient, introvert, self-centred, idealistic or even idle.

The seed of flourishing is latent in the things which naturally walk up to you and not in those to which you run to. Things you would save by a little restraint are worthier than those you will lose through restlessness. A tendency to ignore the closely hidden resources and hunt for the distant ones happens to be the most ancient 'illusive trap' in human history. 'Greed' and 'need' are two different words in the dictionary; but, unfortunately, not so in the human mind. Think carefully, every rat-trap is designed on the basis of 'greed '. If there was no 'greed', there won't be any 'trap'. Effectively therefore, the term 'restraint' was an much an antonym of 'greed' as it was a true synonym of 'evolution'.